THE BIRD WANT EARTH POLLUTION FREE

AARAV DIXIT

Copyright © Aarav Dixit
All Rights Reserved.

This book has been published with all efforts taken to make the material error-free after the consent of the author. However, the author and the publisher do not assume and hereby disclaim any liability to any party for any loss, damage, or disruption caused by errors or omissions, whether such errors or omissions result from negligence, accident, or any other cause.

While every effort has been made to avoid any mistake or omission, this publication is being sold on the condition and understanding that neither the author nor the publishers or printers would be liable in any manner to any person by reason of any mistake or omission in this publication or for any action taken or omitted to be taken or advice rendered or accepted on the basis of this work. For any defect in printing or binding the publishers will be liable only to replace the defective copy by another copy of this work then available.

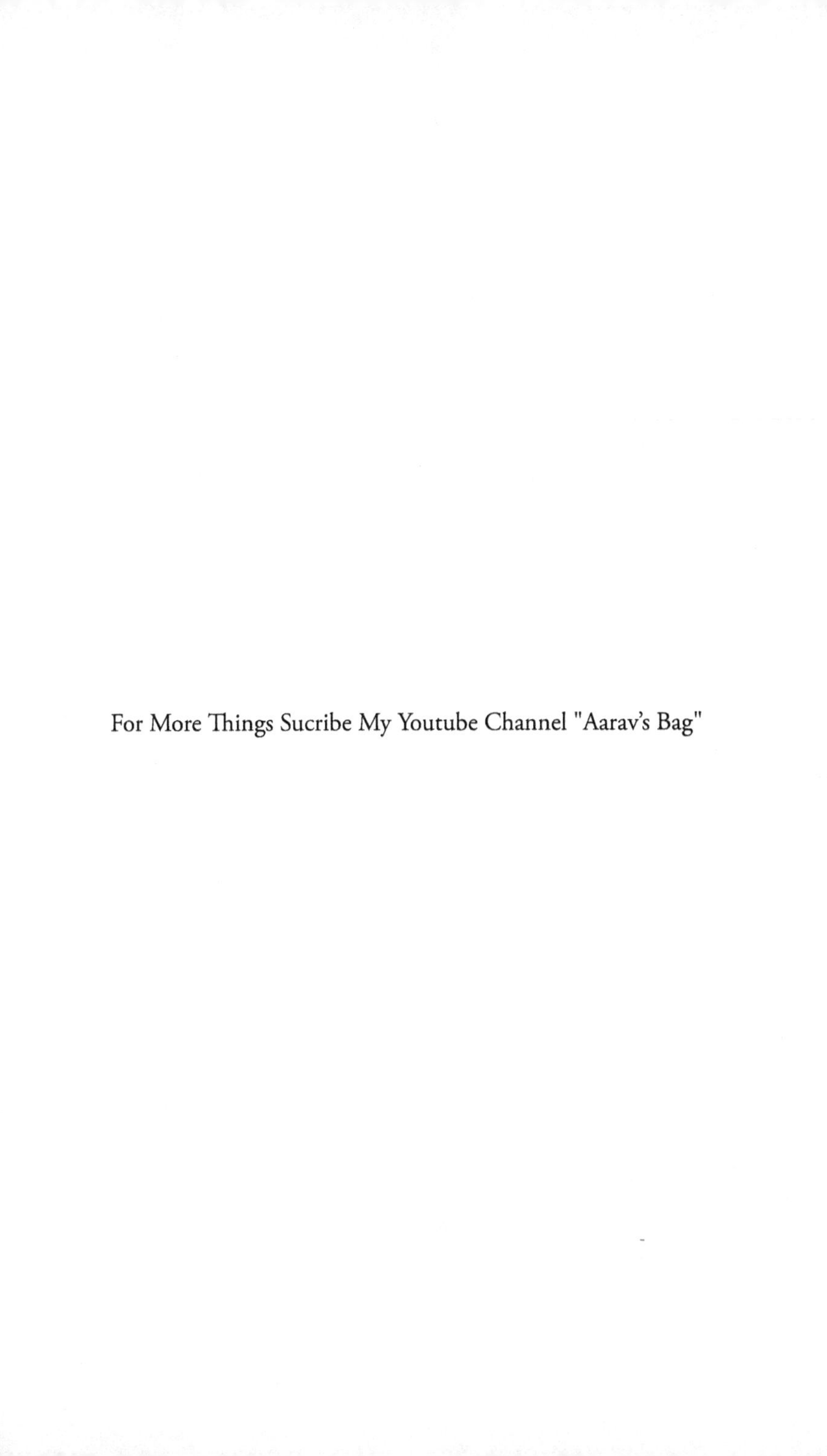

For More Things Sucribe My Youtube Channel "Aarav's Bag"

Contents

Author Bio

I was Born In Jhansi But Curently Living In Noida. I want To be This best selling book of the world. My faroute Subject is Computer. I am Thankfull to Notion Press For Publishing This Book.

Foreword

For More Things Sucribe My Youtube Channel "Aarav's Bag"

Preface

For More Things Sucribe My Youtube Channel "Aarav's Bag"

Acknowledgements

For More Things Sucribe My Youtube Channel "Aarav's Bag"

Prologue

For More Things Sucribe My Youtube Channel "Aarav's Bag"

1. The Bird Want Earth Pollution Free

You'll find me there,
in the land of clean water and air
Where the green grass grows,
Where I feel mud <u>beneath</u> my toes
Where I feel the warmth of bright sun rays,
This is where I wish to spent my days
Where Pollution dose'nt fill up the sky,
Where I can watch birds flying by
This is the place to relax and <u>unwind</u>
This is that gives me peace of wind
Word Meaning:-
Unwind:- *relax after a period of work or tension.*
Beneath:-*at a lower level or layer than.*